# Plantation Princess from Another Planet

For Allison,
Hope it makes
you chuckle!

Love,
Louie

February 2001

# Plantation Princess from Another Planet

## Louise G. Mann

Illustrations by Vicki Hendrix

PHOENIX INTERNATIONAL, INC.
FAYETTEVILLE, ARKANSAS
2000

03 02 01 00    4 3 2 1

Inquiries should be addressed to:

Phoenix International, Inc.
1501 Stubblefield Road
Fayetteville, Arkansas 72703
Phone (501) 521-2204
www.phoenixbase.com


Library of Congress Catalogue Card Number: 00–135371

ISBN 0-9650485-5-1

# Dedication

This silly little book is dedicated to some Yankee friends of mine. These corporate hot-dogs, who found themselves transplanted in the Arkansas Ozarks, were always inviting me to their dinner parties. After a glass of wine I'd start telling stories about my childhood on a plantation in the Delta. My east-coast host requested these embellished tales be put in print and on audio.

So here they are, for my friends who have been baptized in southern culture and renamed Bubba and The Original. Here's to you, sweet friends. Thanks for providing the food, the wine, and best of all, the captive audience! Enjoy and God bless.

# Contents

## Plantation Princess from Another Planet

I think my wayward journey as a plantation princess began with my baptism. I was named after my grandmother, Mary Louise McClintock. But from baptism on, my parents called me Louie. Now how many princesses do you know named Louie? Can you imagine a sixteen-year-old debutante being presented at the country club as "Princess Louie"?

When Robert Lee Wilson, my childhood nemesis,

heard me presented as Princess Louie, he cackled loudly, then yelled, "Hey, is she a cross-dresser?"

I asked my parents why they would call a beautiful baby girl Louie instead of Mary Louise. I was told I had an attitude. What? My mother's doctor listened through his stethoscope and announced, "This baby has an attitude." What a royal welcome for a princess.

A plantation princess has a tremendous burden to bear, trying to live in the past. That is our mission, to carry on southern aristocratic tradition for which there is no place in this new millennium.

Soon after a princess is born she is baptized with a double name like Martha Helen or Sarah Elizabeth. Then for the rest of her life she is called some silly feminine nickname like Precious or Kitten or even Princess.

Social responsibilities begin simultaneously when

the princess enters kindergarten and beauty contests. As she matures she becomes very interested in self-development, of her figure, that is. She will have a training bra by the time she is in fourth grade, bosoms or not. I never did understand how you trained a bosom. Mine never were particularly incorrigible. "Send that breast to reform school."

The princess is participating in modeling class by the sixth grade. Soon thereafter comes cotillion, cheerleading, college, and sororities. When she becomes engaged to a banker or lawyer or better yet the son of a plantation owner, the whole community is expected to come forth and rejoice with expensive gifts: crystal, silver, and linens.

The wedding write-up covers a whole page in the local newspaper. Not only is there media coverage of what everyone wore, but also detailed reports if anyone fainted or threw up at the altar.

After the princess is married she starts making babies and coffeecakes and Rotel cheese dip. In her pantry she will stockpile enough Velveeta cheese to constipate a small army. She is ready to fry chicken and entertain guests at the drop of a hat. These women are bred to hostess and write thank-you notes.

And they don't die for a long time. They do aerobic exercise and get face lifts and tummy tucks and breast implants and liposuction on their thighs. When they finally do go meet their maker, he doesn't recognize them. "Who in the world are you?" asks Saint Peter when they arrive at the Pearly Gate. "This isn't God's image. Whose image is this anyway?"

Well, this was supposed to be my destiny, beauty

contests to a pantry full of Velveeta to liposuction to death. To the outside world my family probably looked appropriate for rearing southern royalty. I guess something must have been amiss genetically, because we certainly did not turn out to be the typical southern aristocratic family.

Daddy did come from plantation stock. He was third-generation cotton farmer and ginner. He was a good Methodist and Rotarian, at church every time the doors were open and at the community house every Tuesday at noon for Rotary.

Momma grew up in Memphis. She attended the appropriate schools, had been crowned Maid of Cotton, and her daddy was a cotton broker. So supposedly she had the right stuff for being a plantation princess.

My folks met in the spring of '51 when Daddy was in Memphis selling the last of the previous year's cotton crop. Granddaddy and my father had gotten to know each other over the years through their cotton transactions.

Granddaddy's office was on Front Street, on the bluff overlooking that wonderful annually out-of-control Mississippi River. Each spring that big ole muddy river busts out of its banks reminding folks that Mother Nature will have the last word.

It is a humbling experience to look down from the Tennessee-Arkansas Bridge and watch that mammoth body of water swallowing up the farmland below. The river would also swallow up the free cobblestone parking spaces along its banks down on Riverside Drive.

Granddaddy was a very practical businessman and

tighter than a tick. He was so tight he even parked on the cobblestones during flooding season. He'd wait 'til the water was lapping at his tires before he'd move the car up to a meter on Front Street.

It only makes sense that the first time my daddy drove into the driveway to pick up my momma for their first date, she was on the roof cementing loose bricks back into the chimney. Any other princess would have been standing on the front porch white gloved and coy, anxiously awaiting the arrival of a gentleman farmer. This should have been a sign of things to come.

My granddaddy wasn't about to pay a professional to repair the chimney when he had help at home who could do the job for free. As Daddy got out of his car Granddaddy bragged out loud, "She's very good with wet cement." Boy, don't you know if my daddy hadn't been interested in going out with her before, he sure was now.

They dated all spring, and in July Daddy proposed. He said ginnin' season was coming up and he couldn't be running back and forth across the river to date so they better get married and get settled in east Arkansas before the cotton crop was ready to be picked.

Duck huntin' season was also approaching, and it required attendance at 4:30 a.m. breakfast gatherings at the American Legion Hut. If a farmer wanted to have any input in the upcoming legislative session he better show up for breakfast.

So, in August of '51 my folks married and set up housekeeping in Shumard. But instead of making coffee-cakes and Rotel cheese dip my momma wanted to go fishin' and duck huntin' and frog giggin'. Folks said she was as peculiar as Daddy's sister, Cappy, who flew an airplane and raised hell as well as horses. Cappy was married to my uncle Sam, a quiet gentle man who of course also farmed. Momma and Cappy would become the best of friends.

During the first year in Shumard, the sisters-in-law did hunt and fish and ride horses all the time. The only way to get Momma or Cappy to show up for a bridge game or social obligation was to hold it at their house.

In the second year Momma got pregnant with my older sister, but that didn't slow her down one bit. She kept right on huntin' and fishin' up 'til the day the baby came. Folks wondered if the baby was going to be born in a hospital or a bass boat.

Aunt Cappy kept telling everyone she would make a great midwife. She kept telling Momma not to worry, if that baby decided to come while they were out in a duck blind she was ready to catch it. Cappy didn't know anymore about birthing babies than Prissy in *Gone with the Wind*.

Much to Daddy's relief, my older sister was born in the community hospital without the assistance of Aunt Cappy. They named the baby after my great aunts Kathryn and Dee Dee. She was supposed to be called Katy Dee, but from baptism on she was called KatyDid.

I was born two years after KatyDid and that was when we moved to the big house on the highway where I began my journey as a wayward plantation princess.

# Bucked Teeth and Beauty Contests

I think the truth was my parents wanted a boy. I think that's why they called me Louie instead of Mary Louise. They wanted a boy until I became a teenager, then they wanted a girl. It's a wonder I'm not a cross-dresser.

My earliest memories are not playing with Barbie dolls or little tea sets. My first toys were fire engines, farm sets, electric trains, and Zorro capes. My earliest memory of a childhood spat is not about dolls or

dress-up clothes. It's a fistfight with Robert Lee Wilson, a chubby Baptist kid who announced to the whole neighborhood that I was going to hell because I was Methodist.

My aunt Cappy, who is Episcopalian, told me you don't have to die to go to hell. She said if you got separated from your soul, you could be alive and walking around on this earth and be in hell. I started keeping my arms close to my chest after that to be sure my soul didn't get loose. As far as going to hell after death, Cappy said there were folks from many different religions who had made reservations with the devil. She said hell was interdenominational.

I didn't think I was going to hell, but I did know I was going to see how many punches I could land upside Robert Lee's head before his momma heard his cries for help. We managed to bloody each other's nose before she pulled us apart.

Mrs. Wilson referred to Robert Lee and me as two holy terrors. I told her if Robert Lee didn't quit threatening me with hell I was going to start a holy war between his Sunday school class and mine. She just shook her head and muttered something about "that evil Cappy's influence on young souls."

While other seven-year-old princesses were attending dance classes and getting prepared for beauty contests I was burning up Highway 83 to Memphis, going to the orthodontist. My front teeth weren't bucked— they were perpendicular to my face.

I thought it was a compliment that Dr. Reynolds referred to me as the greatest challenge of his career. I assumed it meant I was special. Momma said it meant we were paying for his time share in Aspen. He promised to have my teeth straight before my senior prom. My momma said they better be straight before I got out of eighth grade.

Despite the bucked teeth I had a wonderful smile. The only problem was my upper lip was a little short and when I got to laughing real hard my gums would dry out. When the Olin Mills people came to take our school-day pictures the photographer suggested that I shut my mouth. "No way!" I retorted. "My daddy said for what these braces are costing him I better smile and act like I enjoy wearing 'em." I could not have closed my mouth if that man had offered me money. My upper and lower lips had not made physical contact since my two front teeth came in.

Even with bucked teeth a prepubescent plantation

princess was expected to participate in the annual Miss Shumard beauty contest. Aunt Cappy suggested I wear my Zorro cape, which Momma thought would be kinda funny and create quite a stir, but Daddy insisted I go to Memphis and get a new dress for the occasion. I ended up with a little pink frock that had a bunch of lace and bows and made me itch all over.

The night of the pageant I was in a pretty bad mood scratching and itching. It was still daylight outside, and I wanted to be with the neighborhood boys as they headed for the pond to go frog giggin'. Daddy was lecturing me about acting like a lady as I watched Mary Martha Boatwright precede me on stage. Mary Martha's mother, Miss Mary Lee, entered Mary Martha in every beauty contest there ever was. Miss Mary Lee said winning beauty contests could open all kinds of doors. I

just wanted to get out the door, away from the con-
fines of lace and bows, back outside with the boys, the
bugs, and the frogs.

Instead, I was trapped in the Shumard high school
gym in the middle of springtime watching Mary Martha
all dolled up in her red velvet Christmas dress with a big
green bow in her curly blond hair, singing, "All I Want
for Christmas Is My Two Front Teeth." Well, she could
sure as hell have mine and the night brace and retainer
that went with them.

She sang and swayed and beamed like she was
really enjoying herself. The crowd applauded enthusiastically as she made her way to the steps at the side of
the stage. I noticed a big fat cricket on the bottom step.
I reached over and snatched him up. As I passed her
coming down I smiled and told her what a great job she

had done. I also dropped the cricket down the back of her dress.

As Mary Martha went screaming down the steps, Miss Sandy Jones, our tap-dance teacher, nudged me toward the stage. Suddenly I was struck with stage fright. Everyone was looking at my front teeth, and my gums were starting to dry out.

"Go on, honey, you look soooo pretty," Miss Sandy said as she patted me on the back. While walking across the stage looking for the masking tape that marked my place I noticed there in the front row were Uncle Sam and Aunt Cappy. She was beaming proudly and gave me a thumbs up. She had promised to take me for a ride in her airplane after this ordeal was over.

Also on the front row was Robert Lee Wilson, just a snickering.

"Smile!" Miss Sandy whispered from behind the curtain. I had no choice. My gums were totally dried out by now. My upper lip was permanently stuck above my front teeth. As I took my place on the masking tape, Robert Lee hollered out in front of God and everybody, "Hey, Buckedtooth!"

I felt my face turn red as I continued to grin involuntarily. I began to shake with anger. It was bad enough that I was indoors while it was still daylight out and now to have Robert Lee humiliate me in front of half the town. . . . This was more than I could handle.

I lunged toward him just as Miss Sarah Frances started playing the music for my tap-dance routine, "You Are My Sunshine, My Only Sunshine."

I was at the edge of the stage about to pounce Robert Lee when Daddy's eye caught mine. The stern look on his face said "grounding, spanking." Robert Lee continued the bantering, "So crown ole Buckedtooth Miss Shumard." I whispered angrily at Robert Lee that I would crown him later. Then I stomped back over to my masking tape and sang about the damn sunshine.

Sure 'nuff, Mary Martha won the contest, and believe it or not, I came in runner-up. I could not figure out why the judges would name a bucktoothed scrawny-headed tomboy runner-up. Years later I found out it was because Aunt Cappy threatened them. She said I had shown grace under pressure and deserved recognition.

They argued that threatening to beat the stew out of Robert Lee wasn't exactly graceful. Cappy asked them how they would like it if she started flying her plane over their houses at low altitude. That's all she needed to say.

Cappy was hell on wheels and wings. She never did get familiar with the brakes. She knew two speeds, stop and go. Stop usually happened when she hit something.

Those guys who inspect airplane crashes said Cappy had wrecked more times and come up with more creative excuses than any other pilot this century. The judges did not want to risk having Cappy take off a front porch or any other section of their houses so they made me runner-up. Cappy had to promise them I would never ever enter another Miss Shumard beauty contest.

The next day at recess Robert Lee came running by while I was jumping rope. "Hey, Bucktooth!" He giggled as he danced around me. I took that jump-rope and whipped it right across his mouth.

Bloody and crying he went and got Miss Sarah Frances, who escorted us to the principal's office where

Mr. White told me I would apologize. I said I would not. I said I was sorry I only hit him in the mouth, I'd meant to take an ear off as well. Then he'd look like that Van Goat guy we had been studying in Miss Holly's art class.

Mr. White told me I could apologize or he would call my daddy to come down to the school to talk to me. Mr. White knew I'd rather eat nails than have a confrontation with my daddy so I turned to Robert Lee and said I was sorry. When I realized how pleased Mr. White was with my apology, I continued. "Robert Lee, I really really want to be your friend, even though I am a Methodist and headed straight for hell." Mr. White was Baptist so he was doubly pleased that I had acknowledged I was condemned as well as sorry.

Beaming with satisfaction at his mediation skills, Mr. White walked us to the door, patted us each on the shoulder, and told us how proud we'd made him. As soon as we were out of the principal's sight, I whispered in Robert Lee's ear, "You better watch out, good buddy. Next time we go to Mr. White's office together you will be missing an ear!"

## Go-Carts and Mole-Skin Purses

**B**eing banned from beauty contests before the age of seven and a half was not an encouraging sign about my future as a plantation princess. I, however, was delighted to be freed from the bondage of beauty pageants, dance classes, and piano lessons.

My piano teacher, Miss Sarah Frances, had been trying to tell my mother for a year and a half that I belonged outside in the trees not indoors on stage. God bless Miss Sarah Frances, she had a big heart. She was big in other ways as well. She was so wide there was not room for both of us on the piano bench, so she sat and I stood.

When I first began lessons she said we would spend about a month in the primer, *Teaching Little Fingers How to Play*. Eleven grueling months later Miss Sarah Frances announced it was over. It was time for me to be returned to the trees. She made it sound as though I was some endangered monkey that was about to perish in captivity. My mother offered to pay double if she would continue to work with me, but Miss Sarah Frances was not to be swayed.

When Aunt Cappy got word that I'd been thrown out of piano lessons she gave me a go-cart and told me I had a lot of lost time outdoors to make up, so I should ride with great gusto. Cappy was always talking about doing things with great gusto. Uncle Sam, Aunt Cappy's husband, looked weary whenever Cappy brought up the "g" word. I guess a little bit of Cappy's gusto went a long way.

Once released from the shackles of piano lessons I began to spend my afternoons with my maternal grandfather, the retired cotton broker from Memphis. He would come across the Mississippi River several days a week to spend time at his cabin on the lake. He taught me how to put a worm on a hook and tie a fly. We also talked a lot about motors. He said it was important for me to be comfortable with motors before I got a car, that way I would not be taken advantage of by mechanics.

I don't think he really knew much about motors. He

"fixed' my go-cart in such a way that once you turned the engine on you could not turn it off until it ran out of gas. When I asked why he had done that he blamed Aunt Cappy for the stuck accelerator, and she blamed him. Actually, I think Momma did it to keep me outside for hours at a time.

On a hot summer's afternoon I'd drink a big orange and hop on that go-cart, push the throttle full tilt, and head for the neighbor's yard. Mr. Jimma's yard was like an obstacle course with its huge Cherrybark oak trees and mole holes everywhere. If I wasn't dodging a three-foot-wide oak I was swerving past a row of raised dirt where the moles had made a tunnel.

I'd get to laughing so hard I'd have to make a pit stop. Problem was, I could not turn the motor off. So I would go roaring into the garage and slam the go-cart against the back wall. The wheels would be spinning and the motor racing as I made a mad dash into the house.

Bessie, our housekeeper of a thousand years, grew used to this routine and would ask the same question each time I'd exit the bathroom. "Did you make it? If you didn't, then clean up your mess." Sometimes I did and sometimes I didn't. But cleaning up a mess was a small price to pay for such a gigglin' good time.

Our neighborhood consisted of several big ante-bellum houses, each with expansive yards. The community hospital was on the south side of the neighborhood, and it also had a large lawn. As kids we loved to race our bicycles across the lawn and up the emergency-room ramp. If we passed someone on a stretcher going into the hospital we assured the prone patient that Miss Susie, the ER nurse, would fix 'em right up. The paramedics called us the "rolling candy stripers."

Once when my older sister, KatyDid, fell out of the magnolia tree in Mr. Jimma's front yard, instead of going home she rode her bike over to the hospital and up the emergency-room ramp. She knocked on the door, and Miss Susie let her in and put her arm in a cast. KatyDid could ride a bike with no hands so it wasn't a big deal to ride home with a cast on her arm. Momma praised her for handling the emergency in such an efficient manner, and Aunt Cappy took her for a ride in her Cessna airplane.

During the elementary school years I spent a lot of time playing with Bill Ed Moore. He taught me how to throw a football and shoot a BB gun. He also let me ride his little Honda motorcycle. I was never so proud as when we had a wreck and the muffler burned my shin. Too bad I had been banned from beauty contests; they would've been great opportunities to show off my scar.

David Glen was always presenting me with challenges like tying the laces of my saddle oxfords together to see if I could hop all the way home. It took a long time to hop across four acres. He said he would pay me five dollars if I could do it in less than ten minutes.

I'd hop through Mr. Jimma and Miss Clareece's yard. The back door would be open, and I'd hear Miss Clareece cussing at him about urinating in the pantry sink. He had always peed in the pantry sink.

One day Georgia, their cook for a thousand years,

got tired of listening to them fuss about it and suggested they just put a urinal in the pantry. "We know it won't be a waste of money. We know he will use it. That is, unless he just prefers to pee in the sink. What does he use at night when he gets up from the bed? Does he use the sink or the toilet?"

"Well, of course he uses the toilet at night!" Miss Clareece snapped back. But the truth be told I'll bet she didn't really know. I bet after Georgia quizzed her she spied on him to find out. The reason I think that is because it took a while before she finally bought the urinal for the pantry. There it sat, right there at the back door next to the shelf with all the Rotel and canned corn and green beans.

A urinal at the back door made perfect sense to me. I understood what it was like when you got to laughing real hard. There isn't time to go running all through the house looking for a bathroom.

Mr. Jimma and I both liked to laugh real hard; that's why we were such good friends. I asked my parents if we could put a toilet in our pantry, but they said no. Sure would have saved me a lot of trouble.

After finishing his business in the pantry Mr. Jimma came out the back door and saw me struggling with my saddle oxfords. "So you been playing with David Glen? Let's get those shoes retied so you can beat the clock getting home and collect your five dollars." He helped me get my shoestrings untangled and retied.

But before sending me on my way he told me he had an important mission for me. He had captured wild game in his yard and wanted to send it to my parents for supper. He was always doing thoughtful things like that. We went to the garage and got a butterfly net, then walked around to the front yard to one of his mole traps. He was a champion at catching moles.

He carefully dug the trap out of the ground and gently pulled the soft dead mammal off the spike. Then he put the little mole in the butterfly net and told me to take it on home and tell Bessie to make soup with it. He said my daddy could skin it and make me a purse.

I went merrily on my way with the mole in the butterfly net, feeling pretty proud that I was a wild game queen if not a beauty queen. I waltzed into the kitchen where Bessie was fixing supper and dropped my prize on the counter, announcing, "Look what I got."

She turned around and let out a blood-curdlin' scream and started cussin' Mr. Jimma and talking about how crazy he was and about how white people who peed in their pantry when they got a big ole house with four real bathrooms ought to be locked up and the key throwed away.

I rolled my eyes, picked up my wild game and butterfly net, and headed out the door to Aunt Cappy and Uncle Sam's house. But even they did not want mole soup for supper. And I never did get my mole-skin purse.

## Libation

Libation is as much a part of the Delta culture as growing cotton. The liquor closet is as common in a plantation home as a pantry. Our liquor closet was in the hallway coming in from the porch. It was kept locked with the skeleton key hanging on a nail on the doorframe. Some of the contents included Tanqeray gin, Smirnoff vodka, and Johnny Walker Red scotch.

Each night during Walter Cronkite my daddy would fix libation for Momma and himself. He drank the Johnny Walker Red, and she would have a dry martini with three ice cubes and two stuffed olives. They would watch the news, discuss the day's events, and sip.

My maternal grandparents over in Memphis also partook of libation every night, but not my daddy's momma. Grandmother McClintock was a teetotaler. She never touched alcohol, and she did not approve of anyone else touching it either, even on holidays.

As children we realized early on which grown-ups in town drank and which did not. The divisions were usually by religion. The Episcopalians drank openly and theirs seemed to be a generally happy congregation. The Presbyterians also drank openly and they were a pretty congenial group as well. Some of the Methodists drank and some did not, but it didn't seem to matter in their church who preferred to do what.

It was my observation as a little kid that the Baptists were a different story. They said they didn't drink or dance, but I sure saw otherwise whenever I was out at the country club.

Why, it was a bunch of Baptist farmers who boy-cotted the country club when Miss Evelyn raised the price of mixed drinks. They said she was crucifying them with her new prices. They got all mad, and instead of coming indoors for libation, they started parking their pickup trucks at the bottom of the hill, down by the golf-cart houses.

They sat on the tailgates and drank scotch out of Dixie cups. They called themselves "The Excommunicated Saints." Since Baptists don't even have saints, folks questioned their name. The farmers responded that they were sweet as saints and felt like Miss Evelyn had banished them from their club family by setting the liquor prices so high.

The mosquitoes brought those Baptist saints to their knees and ended their boycott. The men said for what they were spending on mosquito repellent they might as well just come back inside. They pleaded with Miss Evelyn to let them back in the clubhouse, promising never to badmouth her again. She said she didn't want them to become a bunch of mosquito-riddled martyrs so she would let them back in. Aunt Cappy said Miss Evelyn was the saint for forgiving their ugly behavior. Cappy said she would have let the mosquitoes eat 'em alive before she would have forgiven them.

But back to Grandmother McClintock. Her disdain for alcohol created an interesting tension in our family during the holiday season. We always spent Christmas Day at her big house on Elm Street. The cousins would come from all around Arkansas, and we had to dress up and act right. The grown-ups would sit at the dining-room table laden with inherited sterling, linen, and crystal. The children were set at a card table off in the corner.

After the older generations took their seats around the massive oval cherry table, my father or uncle would attempt to say grace. Grandmother, deaf but focused, always chose the blessing as the time to lament about Great Aunt Kathryn's shingles.

This also happened weekly during the blessing at Sunday lunch. We would all bow our heads, Daddy would begin, "Lord, make us thankful," only to be interrupted by Grandmother, "Poor Kathryn, poor, poor

Kathryn, shingles, what a curse, what a curse those shingles. . . ."

The kids would get the giggles because we knew that even though Daddy was gonna say, "Mother, I'm trying to pray . . . ," she was gonna say, "Oh, 'xcuse me, son." Then just as soon as he resumed the blessing she was gonna start it up, all over again.

We decided Grandmother's lamenting was an involuntary response to the bowing of her head. She bowed her head, she started to lament. Finally, my daddy and the uncles decided the hell with it, and they learned to pray right on through Grandmother's moaning.

On Christmas Day after lunch and all the gift opening was done, the uncles would sneak outside to swap whiskey. My cousins and I would snicker as our daddys slipped quietly out the front door as though they were on some kind of covert mission. These grown men would huddle behind their cars looking back over their shoulder to be sure no one was watching. We were all watching from the living-room windows.

My uncle would furtively open the trunk of his big white Lincoln Towncar, and Daddy would go behind the seat of his Ford pickup truck. They would pull out bottles of Johnny Walker Red. They were in those tall skinny Christmas bags with the red satin rope handles. They'd laugh and make the swap at the back of Uncle Sam's car. They looked so smug and proud you'd have thought they had just accomplished some great clandestine feat.

By now my cousins and I would have scooted out to Grandmother's front porch to observe this Christmas ritual. It was as traditional as Santa Claus. "Why don't they do this inside when we are unwrapping presents?"

I asked my older cousin, Sam Junior. "Why do they always go out to the driveway?"

He said it was a game they played because they were grown-ups. They liked to think they were pulling something off that Grandmother wouldn't approve of. Meanwhile, she would be standing at the living-room windows peeping through the sheers. She would shake her head in disapproval, then go on back to the kitchen. I never heard her say a word about the annual whiskey swap.

While the uncles were swapping whiskey Momma and Aunt Cappy were hiding in the rose garden smoking Camel cigarettes. They would wait until Grandmother was engrossed at the living-room window then slip a dollar to each of us kids with instructions to "help grandmother clean up." Translated, this meant keep her occupied while they lit up. These annual shenanigans gave us kids a sense of fun holiday tradition.

I thought the grown-ups' antics on Christmas Day were kooky, but not half as kooky as their behavior during a libation raid. One summer evening, when I was six or seven, my little sister and I were taking a bubble bath while the adults were on the porch sipping cocktails.

It's a strict rule in the Delta that children do not bug grown-ups from 5:30 to 7:00 p.m. Libation is a sacred time, kinda like evening prayer. Aunt Cappy even referred to libation as vespers and would make us whisper if we dared set foot on the porch during the hallowed hour. Our parents knew we didn't want to whisper so they could rest assured they would be allowed to sip in peace.

My little sister and I were playin' in a bubble bath

one Saturday night when we heard Aunt Cappy and Momma come racing down the hall. They almost knocked each other down trying to get in the bathroom. They slammed and locked the door.

We giggled as we watched them grab the bar of Ivory soap from the sink and start scrubbing their teeth with their fingers. Then they blew in each other's face and asked, "Do you smell anything?"

My four-year-old sister looked at me quizzically and asked what in the world was going on. I told her I guessed that Grandmother McClintock had just driven in the driveway. This is what happens when she surprises the grown-ups during libation; the women run to the bathroom to wash their mouths out with soap. It's a contest to see if they can do it before she reaches the porch door.

I continued, explaining that this was like a time long, long ago in America. They called this period in history Prohibition. Back then it was against the law for grown-ups to even have libation. I guess the Baptists were running the country.

Anyway, there were people who would go around and do libation raids because they thought drinking was evil. It seemed Prohibition never ended for Grandmother McClintock.

Having been prior witness to this fiasco I guessed that about now Uncle Sam was in the driveway trying to stall Grandmother's entrance while Daddy emptied glasses in the sink and threw the whiskey bottle back in the liquor closet.

It was too bad we were in the bathtub because I had earned fifty cents one time when Aunt Cappy sent me out in the driveway to stall Grandmother. I took her down to the ditch and showed her our treehouse and rope swing. She pretended to be interested, but I knew she had other things on her mind.

I told my little sister when she got older she could probably make some money too. Momma said Prohibition was a wonderful opportunity for American entrepreneurs. There was all kinds of money to be made. Money for people who made the whiskey, for those hiding the whiskey, for those hiring people to do libation raids, for those hiring people to stall the people who were doing the raids. We could pretend we were part of this great American experience as we stalled our grandmother in the front yard.

My sister wanted to know what it was like, washing your mouth out with soap. She knew I had done it once after my first-grade teacher tattled on me for hollering "damn" in the school cafeteria. I was standing in the lunch line when Robert Lee Wilson dropped his tray full of creamed corn all over my new sandals. It was a squishy mess. I almost threw up. I told my teacher if it had happened to her, I bet she would have hollered "damn," too.

Uncle Sam yelled down the hall that the coast was clear. Momma and Aunt Cappy unlocked the door with a sigh of relief and headed back to the porch.

As I look back on my grandmother's libation raid that Saturday night, I bet you dimes to donuts, that while Momma and Aunt Cappy were choking on that bar of Ivory soap, my grandmother got back in her car and giggled to herself all the way home.

## City Cousins

We had these cousins who lived in Memphis. We called them our city cousins. They were nice enough girls, they just didn't know much about climbing trees or getting into mischief. Their daddy, Uncle Harry, was always saying to them, "Respect your elders and do as they say."

The girls were well behaved, shy, easily frightened, and they trusted authority. I liked them anyway and tried to help them with their shortcomings.

Sometimes they would come visit for a weekend

and totally disrupt my routine. Every Sunday morning my siblings and I would go out in the front yard and climb the huge Shumard oak tree. We climbed in our pajamas. I don't know why; I guess it was ritual like going to Sunday school which we would do later in the morning.

One Sunday morning I was trying to help entertain my city cousins. Uncle Harry had dropped them off the night before when he was on his way to Granddaddy's cabin at the lake. I had been told to be nice and to be a good southern hostess and include them in our activities. I intended to integrate them right into our routine.

Sara Lee, the oldest of the three girls, was afraid of heights, always had been. I knew I could help her conquer her fear. I was always helping people, whether they asked for it or not. Often I ended up getting a spanking for my efforts, as well as a lecture to mind my own business and not be making decisions about what was best for other little kids.

But I wasn't easily fazed. I was mission oriented. And my mission this particular weekend was to get my seven-year-old cousin as high up in that Shumard oak tree as I could before she screamed, fell out, fainted or . . . my daddy caught me.

The Shumard oaks in our front yard were about four feet in diameter and tall, tall, tall. Many of the limbs swept down along the ground. I loved those old trees like bosom buddies. They protected me from spankings and BB guns and dogs and piano lessons.

Each time I got in trouble, which was fairly often, I'd head for the oldest oak in the grove. I'd shimmy up those branches like a little monkey. My daddy always said I was part monkey. After I'd reach a certain height none of the grown-ups wanted to mess with me. They knew they might as well just let me alone. I wouldn't be coming down 'til dark.

My little brother was the same way. When Daddy decided to give our two Great Danes away because they had terrorized the neighbor's beagle, my little brother, Walker, climbed up that oak, sat on the same branch I liked to perch on, and did not come down for almost seven hours.

During the day Daddy would ride by the house on his way to the farm and roll down his window and holler, "Come down outa that tree, boy!" Walker would holler back, "Gimme back my dogs."

This went on all day 'til well after dark when I had

to climb up and explain to Walker that Daddy was afraid the dogs might attack some little ole kid. With tears in his eyes Walker said they would never do that, but he reckoned his gerbils were getting hungry so he better come on down and feed them.

But back to my cousin Sara Lee's fear of heights. I knew once I got her up in the nest she would love it and never want to come down. The nest was a huge branch that had lots of little water shoots and leaves all around it. It looked like a prehistoric bird nest. It couldn't have been more than twenty-five or thirty feet up. I thought it would be a great beginning for conquering her phobia.

My first challenge was getting her to wake up. In the country we woke up when the sun came up, probably because we didn't have curtains on our upstairs windows. Momma saw no need to spend money on them because no one could see up to the second floor anyway.

Even with the sun shining in her eyes Sara Lee managed to continue snoring. I nudged and poked her. When that didn't work I went in the bathroom and got a glass of cold water and dribbled it down her face. She jumped up pretty quickly then. I told her I had a great adventure in mind but we had to get going right now or else we couldn't get it done before Sunday school.

Reluctantly she followed me out to the front yard where I pointed to the Shumard oak. "We're just gonna climb a little ways." She said she didn't want to.

"You just think you don't want to, but that's because you're not listening to your heart, which you can't hear in Memphis because the traffic is too loud, which is why it is so important for you to come to the country, so you can listen to me."

She argued a little more, then I bribed her and told her she could have my sister's Barbie doll if she would just get on the lowest branch. It was lying on the ground so there wasn't anything to be afraid of. Once on the branch she seemed to be feeling pretty confident so I was able to nudge her on up to the first branch off the ground. From there I coaxed her up a branch at a time all the way to the nest.

Once in the nest she seemed to be having a good time when Momma yelled that breakfast was ready. I scampered down the tree and raced off to the house. Behind me I heard my city cousin hollering, "Don't leave me. Don't leave me."

As I plopped down to a plate full of silver dollar

pancakes, Daddy asked the whereabouts of Sara Lee. I'd been forewarned not to trick her up into the tree because Daddy knew he would be the one who would have to get her down as well as apologize to Uncle Harry. "Hmm," I pondered. "I don't know where she could be." Daddy glared at me as he headed for the porch door.

By the time he got out to the tree Sara Lee was screaming bloody murder. You'd have thought I'd hung her by her toes. Lord, here I was taking my Sunday morning trying to help her get over a phobia and nobody bothered to thank me. Instead, I got a spanking and a lecture on being a good southern hostess. And then she told Daddy that I'd promised her a Barbie doll that didn't even belong to me. Another spanking.

Aunt Cappy heard about all the trouble I'd gotten

into and as usual came to my defense. She applauded my efforts to help my cousin with her phobia. She encouraged me to keep expanding my city cousin's horizons. She said later in life, Sara Lee would thank me for the memories. Cappy said part of being a great southern hostess was giving your guests memories, and I excelled in that department. No one had ever before referred to me as a great southern hostess.

So later that summer, when the girls came again, I felt obliged to live up to my new reputation. I decided to help the middle cousin, Lizzy Ann, create some memories. (Sara Lee said she'd made all the memories with me she wanted.)

I told Lizzy Ann I was her elder and that she should respect and mind me just like Uncle Harry said. Luckily she went along with the concept which made it pretty easy to coax her into the window seat in my bedroom while we were playing hide-and-seek. I convinced her she should stay there and play a little trick on her daddy. I told her when he came to get her she should be real quiet and see if he could find her.

When Uncle Harry drove up he was so excited about the bass he'd caught he didn't even notice how many kids he was loading in the car. He had Sara Lee and baby Martha Marie, but no Elizabeth Ann. My siblings and I stood in the yard snickering as he drove off. I ran back in the house up to my bedroom to get Lizzy Ann out of the window seat so when he came back she would be out front waiting for him.

When I tried to open the lid to the window seat it gave a little, then slammed shut. Buddy, it was really stuck. Knowing that she would get scared if I admitted I could not get the lid open, I told Lizzy Ann she might want to stay in there just a little longer. I told her the fun was just beginning.

She whimpered that she had had enough fun and she wanted out now. When she really started crying I knew I was probably in for a spanking. I assured her I was going for help and would be back in just a few short minutes. I was really headed for the front yard and the Shumard oak.

Twenty minutes after he departed Uncle Harry came roaring back in the driveway and wanted to know where I was. I was up in the tree wondering if he was going to get all the way back to the city before he realized he was missing a daughter.

And I was wondering how they were going to find her, since I sure wasn't going to confess that I'd put her in the window seat with a stuck lid. If she suffocated before they found her, I was liable to get grounded as well as spanked.

When he demanded to know her whereabouts I shrugged and hollered from the old oak, "Beats me, you know how your girls seem to always be getting into mischief."

"I'll mischief you!" he yelled back up.

I tried to think what Cappy would do under the circumstances. She would probably lead them to the scene of the crime but not confess, until caught.

I told Uncle Harry that the last time I saw Lizzy Ann we were playing hide-and-seek so I suspected she might be somewhere in the house. It took 'em a while to find her. My uncle was upstairs looking under beds when he heard a muffled cry from the window seat, "Hep me, hep me, get me outa here. . . ."

By the time they got her out I was clear up in the top of the old Shumard. My daddy stood at the bottom hollering at me until my uncle's car was outa sight. I yelled back that I was just helping my cousin make memories. He told me I was going to remember the spanking I was going to get just as soon as I came down outa that tree. I learned that summer what a tremendous burden great southern hostesses bear.

I thought I was through being burdened, until the last week of summer when Uncle Harry came by with baby cousin Martha Marie. She was only two and tiny for her age. My sisters and I were told to look after her while she napped.

Uncle Harry felt we could do her no harm just looking at her. So we looked and looked and looked as she slept on my sister's bed. And as we looked at her I noted that she was about the same size as the teddy bear in my sister KatyDid's bottom drawer.

KatyDid's chest of drawers was built into the wall. Upon pulling out the bottom drawer to get the teddy bear I remarked how the bear had been in the wall.

What if we put Martha Marie in the bottom drawer and pushed it back in, then pulled out the other three drawers . . . ? We would be watching her in the wall. What a great memory. When she grew up she could tell her friends how she took a nap in a drawer in the wall. My sisters agreed it was a great idea.

So we pulled out the bottom drawer and made a little bed with a towel. We managed to place her in the drawer before she woke up. "Quick, shut the drawer!" I whispered as she began to stretch and yawn.

Next we pulled all the drawers above her out so we could see her and talk to her. She woke up, but wasn't frightened. She stood up and waved and giggled. We found this entertaining for a while, then got bored and told her to lie down so we could get her out of the wall.

I don't know if that baby was stubborn or really just didn't understand, but she would not lie down. After having gotten two spankings that summer for trying to help my city cousins expand their horizons and make memories there was no way I was taking the rap for this one. I went on outside and ran down to the ditch to play on the rope swing.

As I was sailing over the ditch thinking up my alibi, I saw Momma's station wagon pull in the driveway. My sisters came running out to meet her and tell on me. They said that I had put Martha Marie in the wall, then gone to the ditch to act like I wasn't any part of it, but really the whole thing was my idea.

Momma came charging down to the ditch and told me if I ever wanted to ride my go-cart again I'd better get in that house and get that baby out of the wall before her daddy arrived. She was hollering about what was wrong with us kids to treat our cousins so bad.

By the time I got upstairs Martha Marie had gotten tired and lay down again, and my sisters were pulling her out of the drawer.

They had just put her on the bed when Uncle Harry appeared at the porch door. I met him coming up the stairs. "Well, I didn't see Martha Marie stranded in the oak out front so I figured you've put her in the window seat to take her nap."

"No, sir," I assured him, "she took her nap in the bottom drawer of the dresser." He raced passed me up the stairs, and I raced out the door, beaming with pride that once again I had lived up to my reputation as a great southern hostess.

# Bare Chests and Burning Cows

The plantation princesses all have their coming-of-age stories, like purchasing their first brassiere, how their mother took them to be fitted, what an exciting mother-daughter event it was. You know, one of those bonding experiences.

My mother and I bonded over the John Deere tractor we used to cut our four-acre yard. It was her first anniversary gift from my daddy, and she kept it running for more than three decades.

While other girls were talking with their mommas

about breasts, my momma and Aunt Cappy were teaching me that you must change the oil in any engine regularly, and when you change the oil, you must also change the oil filter. "Clean oil is the lifeblood of an engine," they concluded. Nonetheless, I do have a story about that first bra.

It was a beautiful Sunday morning back in the spring of 1965. I was in fifth grade. We were at Sunday school when my daddy and little brother came racing in to get my sisters and me. Daddy was all excited and said we had to go right then. It was a rare event when my daddy would take us out of Sunday school so I knew something very important was going on.

It turned out that some of the farmhands had been burning a dead cow the afternoon before and had gone off and left the fire unattended. During the night the fire got outa hand and now half a pasture was ablaze. The fire department wanted fifty dollars to go outside the city limits to put it out.

Aunt Cappy offered to fly over and dump some kind of chemical on it, but the chemical was even more expensive than the fire department. Really, Daddy was afraid Cappy would get so caught up in the excitement that she would crash and start another fire. Momma said it was ridiculous to pay for the fire department or the chemicals when she had four able-bodied kids who could sling wet gunnysacks.

So my parents took us home, and we threw off our dresses, lacy white socks, and patent leather shoes. We jumped into shorts and tee shirts, got our gunnysacks, and off we went.

Actually, my five-year-old brother, Walker, was

undressed, down to his underwear, before we got in the driveway. It was a game we played with him weekly after church. We'd tease him about how when we got home we were gonna get undressed and be outside climbing trees before he had even got his Sunday shoes off.

Being the youngest was not easy for the only boy in the family. Walker decided the best way to keep from being left behind was to get a head start, so he'd begin taking his clothes off at church, as soon as he was done shaking the minister's hand.

When Miss Kathy Sue, the choir director, reported to Momma that Walker was in the parking lot unzipping his pants, Momma put her foot down. She said there would be no disrobing outside the car. On second thought, Walker was not to take off an article of clothing until an adult had turned on the engine.

After church Walker would race to the front of the line, shake the minister's hand, and run out the door. Brother Bill asked Daddy why Walker was always in such a hurry to leave the church. Daddy said that boy was so inspired that he just couldn't wait to spread the gospel. Brother Bill beamed. Daddy didn't say that the gospel according to Walker was to get naked as soon as you got in the car.

When Momma cranked up the old Ford station wagon Walker began to strip. He'd undo that little bitty tie, rip off that 100% cotton shirt. Yep, by the time we hit our driveway he'd be barefooted, in his underwear.

The Sunday morning we were going to put out the

pasture fire Daddy hollered at us to begin undressing, even before Momma started the car. We were unzipping our dresses, feeling like we were in a scene from "Mission Impossible" where every minute was critical. Walker was squealing with delight. Momma said to hold up, just hold up. She didn't want to be leaving the church parking lot with a car full of naked children.

By the time we got home, changed clothes, and got out to the farm, the fire had spread across our pasture and into the Anderson's property. To no one's surprise Aunt Cappy was flying overhead radioing containment reports to Uncle Sam. He had pulled up in his pickup truck with lemonade, buckets of water, rags, and more gunnysacks in the back. I could tell this was going to be a rip-roarin' good time.

A bunch of the farmhands were fighting the fire on

the south side of the pasture so we were assigned the perimeter. Daddy said our mission was containment. That meant we were not to get near the center of the flame, but rather go after the little stuff on the edges. He gave each of us a gunnysack and told us to drench them in the pond and then go beat that fire. KatyDid got so excited about our mission that she fell in the pond while getting her gunnysack wet. She pulled herself up laughing and went skipping happily across the pasture.

Uncle Sam put Walker in the back end of his truck and told him he had the most important job of all, passing out the lemonade. Walker was barefooted, in his shorts, and beaming. He probably spilt as much lemonade as he poured. But he was great at soaking rags in the bucket and tossing them to the fellas as they approached the truck to get a drink and cool off.

After about an hour of beatin' flames I was gettin' pretty hot, so I took off my shirt. All the guys had their shirts off so I didn't think much about it.

Next thing you know, here comes my momma runnin' and screamin' across acres of blazing pasture. I couldn't tell what she was hollerin', but, boy, did she look mad. As she approached me, I heard her yell, "Put that shirt back on right now. What do you think you are doing running around half-naked in a pasture full of men? You're worse than your little brother. What is wrong with you kids?"

She and I had been arguing for weeks about getting me a training brassiere. Every other girl in fifth grade had one. She said she wasn't gonna spend money on a bra until I had something to train. I kept telling her they wouldn't grow without something to catch 'em as they came springing from my chest.

So there we were . . . standing in the midst of this flaming pasture, with this big ole charred Black Angus cow, me baring my flat little chest and her red faced and screaming, encircled by wide-eyed men holding wet gunnysacks with Aunt Cappy flying overhead.

I calmly responded to her hysteria, "If I'm too little to have a brassiere then I'm little enough to go without a shirt."

We got the fire put out that afternoon, and I got my first brassiere the next day.

# The Turquoise Toilet

While New England celebrates the golden colors of fall, the oranges and yellows of the maple trees, in the Delta, white is the color for autumn. When the cotton bolls burst open, the summer green fields are transformed into a vast sea of white fluff.

Used to, field hands would walk the rows, pull the cotton from the stalk, and drop it into the long burlap bags they drug behind them. Nowadays, the cotton is removed by big machines, appropriately named, cotton pickers.

After the cotton is dumped from the cotton picker into a tall rectangular metal box, it is compacted from the top. It is compacted so tightly that when the sides of the box are removed it holds its shape, looking like a mammoth-size loaf of Wonder bread.

A tarp is pulled over this huge white mass, and later it is pulled by cleated endless chains into a truck and taken from the field to the cotton gin. When I was growing up cotton was transported from the field in big wire-sided trailers.

There was a continual parade of these trailers making their way into town from September until after Christmas. Scraps of cotton littered the highway from the various farms all the way to the gin. The town would be veiled by a layer of lint during ginnin' season.

The cotton gin is the machine that separates the cotton fiber from the seed. Most people give Eli Whitney credit for inventing the gin. I think it was probably invented by an African guy who spent day after day pulling the fiber from the boll. Whoever invented it, it's a very interesting process to observe.

Nowadays, there is a room with a big computer controlling the whole operation. The new machinery can read moisture levels as well as lint content. The trucks carrying the cotton to the gin are weighed twice, once when they first arrive full and again after they've been emptied.

As kids my siblings and I would walk along the highway in front of our house picking up scraps of cotton that had blown off the trailers. We'd pick a paper sack full, take it down to the gin, and get on the truck scales and holler, "Hey, weigh us in!"

Aunt Cappy usually worked the scales during ginnin' season. She would give each of us a nickel for our sacks and tell us not to spend it all in the same place. We thought we were gettin' rich, and Momma was delighted to have the front yard picked up.

I also enjoyed ginnin' season because we got to go out to the farm at night and watch the cotton pickers working in the dark. We'd sit on the steps of the headquarters store and look down into the fields for miles. The pickers looked like mechanical ants marching in lines with their headlights beaming out into the rows of brown stalks and white fluff.

On the way back into town Daddy would turn off

the highway and drive along the levy. He'd stop and we would all lie in the back of the truck and look at the stars. Without the glare of town lights we could see the constellation Orion.

Since Daddy always worked late during this season he'd often swing by the house around supper time and pick up one of us kids to go with him to the gin. We loved to go and play in the overflow, a three-sided box with walls fourteen feet high. The overflow captured the excess cotton that fell from the conveyer belt overhead.

We could be entertained for hours bouncing around that bin full of cotton. Aunt Cappy used to get in the overflow with us. She would chase after us with the big vacuum pipe that was used to suck the cotton back up into the system. She said we were gonna be sucked up and pressed into a bale. We'd squeal and throw arm loads of the white stuff at her.

One night about 6:30 Daddy came by and picked up my little brother to go with him to the gin. Walker was probably about three or four at the time, and he loved to play in the overflow. He was delighted to escape the supper table for this adventure.

Two hours later, when Daddy returned, we noticed Walker wasn't with him. He often forgot Walker. Actually, he had a reputation for forgetting all of his children. It didn't scare us being left around town occasionally. We knew we were supposed to shake hands and introduce ourselves wherever we were, regardless of the circumstances. Folks in Shumard were real nice about bringing us home when we got abandoned.

This particular night when he walked in the door and we asked where Walker was, Daddy froze. The overflow, with a hulking vacuum pipe, was probably not the best place to leave a little bitty kid. My mother was shaking her head and saying her only boy was probably being sucked up into the baler right this moment.

My sisters and I were giggling about how Walker would look if he got pressed into a bale of cotton. I was trying to imagine if his feet would be at the bottom of the bale or stuck out the sides. I've never seen my father move so fast as when he shot out the door that night.

Of course when he got to the gin one of the guys was in the overflow playing with my little brother. Robert had the pipe just above Walker's head sucking his hair straight up. They were laughing and having a good time. "Making memories," that's what Daddy would say about the adventures we had with him. He was a good southern host.

Another special thing about ginning season was that with all the extra help there was a need for extra bathrooms. Daddy would rent a couple of those turquoise porta potties. Not only did they provide relief for the "gin hands" but also for the local winos who wandered by after making a purchase at the liquor store across the street.

When the season was over someone would take the potties out to the farm and clean them up before turning them back in. Only one year somehow one of the turquoise porta potties was forgotten. It must have sat on the gin lot for six months without being emptied.

One Saturday morning Daddy was sitting reading the paper when he suddenly remembered the potty and decided it had to be dealt with at that instant. He hopped into his truck and took off without a word.

When he arrived at the gin, a couple of winos, Otis and Avis, were weaving their way across the street from the liquor store. Daddy solicited their help in lifting the turquoise toilet into the back end of his truck. Obviously after six months it was pretty heavy and man oh man did it smell!

Lifting the potty was quite a challenge because Avis and Otis had already had their morning libation and Daddy has inner ear problems, which affect his balance.

Somehow, without mishap, the tottering trio engineered the turquoise toilet into the bed of the truck. Feeling rather cocky for having accomplished this balancing act, the unsteady threesome squeezed into the front seat and proceeded down Cherry Street.

Cherry has a steep incline about a block from the gin, in front of the A1 Laundry Mat, which was celebrating its grand reopening. It had burned to the ground six months earlier and was just now reopening for business. As they approached the A1, Daddy noticed all the folks coming in and out and decided to stop and congratulate the proud owner, Eldon Brice.

Daddy, like Aunt Cappy, doesn't use his brakes very often. They say they don't want to wear them out too fast. But when they do brake it is with great gusto. Not thinking about the turquoise toilet in the back of the truck Daddy stomped the brake while hollering, "Congratulations, Eldon!"

Boom! The porta potty slammed to on its side and slid out of the truck. It landed upright with the door wide open and six months' worth of stuff oozing out right there at the grand reopening of the A1 Laundry Mat.

Mr. Brice was fit to be tied. Daddy, red faced and flustered, shoved Avis and Otis out of the cab, gave them each five dollars, and told them to guard the potty while he went for help.

They took the money and told him they would be happy to guard the porta potty while he went for help but they really didn't think anyone wanted to get near it so he didn't need to worry too much that it was going to get "stole."

Daddy jumped back in the truck and took off as Mr. Brice stood shaking his head in disgust. Of all the days.

My daddy didn't have a clue what he was was going to do to remedy the situation. He just wanted to get the hell away from the scene of the crime. He cruised up town around the square trying to collect his thoughts. When he passed the fire hall and saw a couple of guys sitting out front spitting tobacco into #10 vegetable cans he decided he had just the project for them.

The firemen really got into the spirit of the grand reopening, turning on the fire truck sirens as they headed down Cherry Street. Sam Hughes, across the square at the radio station, was kinda confused and got on the air announcing that the A1 was on fire again.

By the time Daddy got back down to the laundry mat half the town was there. Avis and Otis looked a little disoriented as the fire engine came roaring up and the fellows jumped off pointing hoses in their direction. Avis swore they did not steal the porta potty and put it in the middle of the road. They were being paid to guard it, he exclaimed. Mr. Brice threw up his hands as the crowd fell out laughing and the firemen began to hose the mess off the street.

I don't imagine this was exactly the way Mr. Brice envisioned his grand reopening. But as Daddy drove away with the porta potty back in his pickup truck and the two winos in the cab beside him, he hollered over his shoulder, "Making memories, Eldon, making memories."

# Alligators, Skunks, and Senators

Everybody in the Delta has pets. No plantation would be complete without them. While the other plantation princesses around me usually had a beautiful cat or a collie or maybe even a peacock wandering the grounds, we had alligators, a skunk, gerbils, and fawn-colored Great Danes.

Daddy brought the alligators home after a meeting with a group of farmers. They had decided to use the reptiles to get rid of the beavers that were causing flooding problems on several fields. They were just little bitty things, and Daddy was going to take them to the farm when they got bigger.

I knew Bessie wasn't going to like this one bit. She had already threatened to quit when Momma let the Great Danes become indoor dogs. Bessie said it was like having deer running loose in the house.

Walker would let the alligators out of their cages when no one was paying attention. One morning, I heard Bessie scream from the living room. She had been vacuuming under a sofa when two little alligators came slithering out. They had their mouths open, hissing at her, as she yelled, "I'll make me a belt out of you before you ever get to the farm."

Walker thought they needed to be outside anyway, so he snuck them over to Mr. Jimma's yard where they could swim in his goldfish pond. They had a great time and ate every one of Mr. Jimma's goldfish. That's when we got the skunk.

Mr. Jimma and my momma were always playing practical jokes on each other. One Halloween, he sent a broom over with a note that read, "Ride, girl, ride." She responded by sending him a cheese ball for his Halloween party. Only it wasn't really a cheese ball. It was a tennis ball covered in port wine cheese and pecans.

So when the alligators ate all Mr. Jimma's goldfish, he made a special trip to Memphis to buy this descented skunk from one of those pet shops that sells unusual pets. Of course, when he brought it over he didn't say it was descented.

Unfortunately, Bessie answered the door when the skunk arrived. I heard her exclaim, "Sweet Jesus, deliver me!" Mr. Jimma announced he was bringing pet food for those damn alligators . . . and, by the way, we owed him some goldfish.

He told Bessie if she would keep her cool and talk only in whispers, the skunk would not spray anyone. Momma and Daddy and Uncle Sam and Aunt Cappy were away on a trip, so poor Bessie was left to deal with us kids, two Great Danes, a couple of gerbils, alligators, and now a skunk that wouldn't spray as long as we talked in whispers.

Why she didn't quit that day I'll never understand. We made up a version of hide-and-seek using the skunk. I took the skunk in his cage and hid him in my momma's closet among her shoes. My siblings tippy-toed around my parents' bedroom trying to guess where he had been hidden. I would whisper, "Cold, cold," as they walked away from the closet. Meanwhile, I was inching my way out the door so when they got close to the closet I could holler, "Hot!" and run down the hall, leaving them to get sprayed.

Bessie cut a switch and threatened us with our lives if we raised our voices one more time before our parents returned. That was the quietest four days we ever spent.

Aunt Cappy had given Walker four gerbils for his sixth birthday. At night when he was in the bathtub, Walker would put those little rodents in a round cake pan and let them float in the tub while he was bathing. If they made little droppings, he'd flip the pan over and give them a bath.

He loved one gerbil in particular, Charlie Brown. Charlie Brown was missing a leg but managed to get around okay on the other three. Walker would take him out of his cage and let him run around on the porch. One afternoon, Walker and his buddy Davis were playing with Charlie Brown on the wicker table on the porch. He was scurrying around when one of the Great Danes came bounding through the screen door.

In a flash, that dog opened his mouth and Charlie Brown disappeared in the folds of the canine's huge tongue. Walker yelled at Davis, "Open his mouth! Hold it open!" Davis grabbed the dog by the jaws and pried his mouth open as Walker reached in for Charlie Brown's tail. "Got it!" He screamed triumphantly as he pulled the gerbil back to daylight.

Slimy and shook up, Charlie Brown survived his Jonah experience. Miss Shirley wrote about it in her "Around Town" column. She said it was a remarkable experience and described it like one of those 911 rescues you see on TV.

Bessie said that it was a crying shame the Great Danes didn't eat the gerbils, the skunk, and the alligators. She said she was tired of vacuuming around wild animals, made her feel like a zookeeper instead of a housekeeper.

The Great Danes along with Walker and Davis could really stir up some mischief. One afternoon, Walker and Davis asked Bessie how to get to China. She told them it was on the other side of the world so the most direct route would be to dig a tunnel.

Which is what they decided to do. They got some shovels and started digging a hole under the treehouse in the back yard. They planned to jump from the treehouse straight through to China.

After the boys began shoveling dirt, the dogs got interested and started digging along with them. By the time Momma got home that afternoon, they had dug a hole about four feet deep and five or six feet wide. They had also dug up two hundred jonquil bulbs in the process. Thinking they were onions the boys put them in a wagon and brought them up to the kitchen door so Bessie could use them. Bessie just shook her head and sighed. "Oh Lord."

The next morning as Momma climbed up on the little bulldozer she rented to fill in the hole, the boys looked at each other tearfully, saying, "And we were so close to China."

That wasn't the only international experience the dogs would have. The illustrious Senator Fulburn came through Shumard that fall, and Daddy invited him to stay at our house. The senator from northwest Arkansas was well known for his international efforts. He had become such a prestigious statesman that a scholarship at the university had been created in his honor.

We were told to be on our best behavior and not create any trouble. I intended to live up to my reputation as a great southern hostess. During dinner, as the grown-ups talked about politics and foreign relations, something came up about China. Walker interrupted the discussion to tell the senator that he almost went to China one time, but Momma got a bulldozer and closed off the route. Senator Fulburn told Walker not to worry, Richard Nixon was going to open the routes back up. Walker beamed with excitement.

Aunt Cappy and Uncle Sam came to the reception held later that evening in our living room. Uncle Sam asked the senator how things were going in Washington with all the furor over the Vietnam war. The senator had taken quite a beating by denouncing the war.

Cappy, with a twinkle in her eye, asked if he sometimes felt like he was in a den of alligators when he was on the Senate floor. The honorable senator nodded and said that was exactly the reason he enjoyed getting back to his home state. He especially enjoyed trips to rural areas like ours where he could relax and enjoy the calm. She smiled and said she was sure his visit here would be memorable.

Everything was calm until the senator went to bed. About half an hour after he said good night and closed the door to the guestroom, we heard a commotion.

"Get out of my bed!" the senator bellowed. Daddy went racing down the hall and into the guest room to find the two Great Danes up in the bed with the congressman. Senator Fulburn was actually kinda laughing about the kooky situation when Walker appeared announcing that his alligators were missing.

Behind Walker were KatyDid and my little sister looking for Stinky, the descented skunk. "I wonder who let all the creatures loose," Momma mused while glaring at me. "Hmm," I pondered as I tried to avoid her eyes.

As Daddy and the senator were pulling the Great Danes off the bed, we heard a skirmish under the bed. An alligator came running out and bit the senator's toe. Hot on the heels, well, tail, of that alligator was Stinky and behind the skunk, another alligator.

The Great Danes went racing down the hall chasing after the skunk and slithering reptiles. My siblings and I chased the Great Danes. Meanwhile, the senator hastily packed his bags and limped out to his car. When Daddy asked where he was going, Senator Fulburn responded, "Back to DC, where at least the alligators are confined to the halls of Congress!"

# A New Pickup Truck Isn't Broken-in until You've Totaled It

**W**hen my cousin Sam Junior turned sixteen and got his first pickup truck we all wondered how long it would take before he wrecked it. We wondered if Sam had his momma's or his daddy's driving genes. If he had Aunt Cappy's genes that truck was liable to be dented up before he ever drove it off the lot. If he had Uncle Sam's genes he would drive it for ten years and never get a scratch on it.

Turned out he had both. He drove as carefully as

his daddy, but his new pickup truck got smashed up anyway. Bless his heart, he was on his way to school on a rainy morning when he stopped at the red light.

Problem was, the guy behind him didn't stop. Sam's brand-new truck was pushed into the guy in front of him who was pushed into the guy in front of him. Yep, a four-car pileup. Most exciting thing that had happened in Shumard in months. The fire engines came racing from the town square, as did the newspaper crew. They were just thrilled to have a picture of a four-car pileup. Shumard only has one stoplight, so it didn't take very long for everyone to arrive at the scene of the accident.

Poor Sam, he was distraught. His truck looked kinda like an accordion. When Cappy arrived she told him not to worry, as far as she was concerned he was just getting that truck broke-in. "That truck," Officer Wallace mumbled to himself, "is totaled." To say Aunt Cappy firmly believed that a new vehicle needed to be broken-in was an understatement.

As kids, we would gather in the garage on our tricycles, bicycles, little Texaco trucks, and fire engines and ram into each other, screaming, "Watch out, Aunt Cappy's driving!" Bessie would come to the porch door and tell us to quit hollering Aunt Cappy's name. It wasn't respectful. It wasn't that we didn't respect her: We loved her dearly. But damn, she was the worst driver Shumard had ever produced.

Aunt Cappy was hell on wheels. She was also a speed demon. One time, going to and from Memphis, she got two tickets in the same day at the same place. The officer who wrote her up said she had become a line item in the state police annual budget. She took it as a compliment when he said she was their most reliable source of income.

Another time, she tried to outrun a state trooper, and when he caught her she chewed him out, telling him he was going to make her late to the church bazaar. The trooper patiently responded, "Miss Cappy, I'm writing this ticket as fast as I can."

She was also a legend among the local police. The third time she ran over the drive-by mailbox out back of the post office, Mr. Brown, the postmaster, banned her from using it. This meant she had to parallel park on Main Street.

One morning while trying to parallel park, she creamed three cars. She was so disgusted she just went on home without even picking up her mail. The owners of the cars, including Eldon Brice, were inside fussing at

Mr. Brown, saying it would be less expensive to continually replace the drive-by mailbox than it would be to repair two and three automobiles a day.

Aunt Cappy had not bothered to exchange insurance information or anything. She just went on home even before the police arrived. When the officer came to the house to talk to her, he mentioned that she had left the scene of an accident. Annoyed, she admonished him, "Now, James Wallace, I knew you knew where I lived, and I saw no point in blocking traffic."

Officer Wallace had better things to do than fuss with Aunt Cappy, so he just wrote up the ticket and told her how pretty her rose garden was lookin' this year. She stuck the officer's report in her denim jacket pocket, then headed out to the garden where she cut a beautiful bouquet for him to take home to his wife.

Aunt Cappy did not approve of the one and only stoplight in Shumard. She said it wasn't environmentally responsible. Not many people were thinking about the environment way back then, but Cappy was. She said sitting there burning up gas when there was no one else in sight was wasteful and she wanted no part of such nonsense.

Uncle Sam tried to explain to her that stopping for a red light was the law. She said it went against nature's laws. Shumard citizens knew to watch out for Cappy at the intersection, but of course, out-of-towners weren't aware of her stoplight boycott. As she approached the intersection, Cappy would slow down. If she didn't see anyone coming from the perpendicular directions, or Officer Wallace, then she would just go right on through that red light.

Cappy got in big trouble when some out-of-towner sideswiped her at the light totaling both vehicles. When Officer Wallace drove up, Cappy was lambasting this poor addled driver for speeding through our little community, "where," she pronounced, "pedestrians have the right of way!"

Pedestrians were safe only if they were agile enough to jump out of Cappy's way. Why she was talking about pedestrians was a mystery. There weren't any pedestrians involved in this accident. Officer Wallace accused her of trying to change the subject. The out-of-towner was cited for speeding and he got a ticket. Cappy got her license taken away for six months and had to go to driver's education.

She spent several Saturdays driving around the high school parking lot with Officer Wallace teaching her how to use the brakes. She didn't approve of brakes much more than she did that stoplight. She insisted she had never had a problem stopping her truck. James Wallace agreed that she usually did come to a stop—when she hit something.

But the law required that she come to a stop without totaling her vehicle or someone else's. "The law," she muttered as she brought the truck to a screeching halt, almost throwing James through the windshield.

When she finally did pass the driver's ed class Uncle Sam bought her a bright yellow Ford pickup truck. He thought a bright color might keep her out of trouble since folks could spot her from a distance. Hopefully they would just get off the road before she reached them.

She loved that new yellow truck. She would hop in

it and head out to the farm and invariably get stuck while taking shortcuts in places she wasn't supposed to be. Then she would get on the radio to Mr. Sims, owner of the local gas station. Seems like every other day he was taking his wrecker to pull her out of some ditch or field.

It got so anyone looking for Aunt Cappy would just call Mr. Sims and he would identify which field she was stuck in that day. I think she became a line item on Mr. Sims's budget also.

One afternoon during a drought summer he got a call from Cappy suggesting he invite the fire department to join him in rescuing her. When he asked what was going on she said not much, just that she had gotten stuck in a cornfield and spun the wheels quite a bit and set the field on fire. She said she was getting awfully hot so if he would please bring a big orange drink when he came out she sure would appreciate it.

The fire department, Mr. Sims, and the newspaper reporters all appeared on that scene. Aunt Cappy burned up that whole field of corn. It didn't do her truck much good either. She rationalized the situation by saying corn prices were so bad that year it didn't matter anyway.

When we'd see Cappy pull in our driveway in her bright yellow beat-all-to-hell pickup truck, we tried to guess about the latest accident. There might be a door or a tailgate missing. When we quizzed her about these mishaps, she'd shake her head and say they weren't her fault, they could've happened to anyone. Once when I asked her about a smashed-in windshield, she declared she had been hit by a big damn Delta mosquito.

While they were building their big house out on the farm, Aunt Cappy and Uncle Sam lived next door to Grandmother McClintock. They shared Grandmother's garage until Cappy got her truck bumper tangled up with Grandmother's Impala bumper so badly that Mr. Sims had to come pull the bumpers off both vehicles to get them apart. He said when it came to car crashes and mishaps Aunt Cappy was a creative genius. Grandmother said the creative genius could just park her bright yellow metal heap elsewhere.

Parking the truck wasn't Cappy's greatest skill. One time she left it running when she went in to the country club to pick up a platter for the church supper. The clubhouse set atop one of the few hills in Shumard. Down below were the golf-cart houses. As Aunt Cappy stood in the kitchen talking to Miss Evelyn, Miss Mary

Lee walked in and asked Cappy if that was her truck out front. She answered yes. Did she leave it in park? Miss Mary Lee continued.

As Cappy raced out of the kitchen, Miss Mary Lee told Miss Evelyn to look out the window. Apparently, Aunt Cappy's truck had been in neutral and had rolled down the hill and slammed into Eldon Brice's golf-cart house. Miss Mary Lee said it popped that golf cart out the backside, like a cork out of a champagne bottle. Mr. Brice's golf cart was in the ditch behind the shed with Aunt Cappy's pickup truck square on top of it.

As Eldon Brice and Cappy stood over the ditch watching Mr. Sims pull the mangled vehicles out, Mr. Brice commented, "Well, Cappy, I think you've got this pickup truck pretty well broke-in."

## One-Bosomed Women

My aunt Cappy probably was my favorite role model. Her wit and courage couldn't be beat, especially in the face of adversity.

Like many women in my momma's circle, Cappy had only one bosom. God gave her two, but cancer took one. Uncle Sam, being the loyal, kind man that he is, was right there when they wheeled her out of surgery. He wanted to be the one to tell her about the cancer.

Since Aunt Cappy was a pilot, Uncle Sam broke the

news of the mastectomy by saying, "Well, Cap, we're now flying on one wing." She grinned at him and answered, "I can fly with one wing if you can." He smiled and kissed her forehead and off she went to the recovery room.

The nurses in the hospital loved having Cappy as their patient because her attitude was so upbeat. Instead of feeling sorry for herself about losing a wing she told everybody who came to visit how very grateful she was for early detection because it had definitely saved her life. She probably saved the lives of dozens of other women over the years when she convinced them to go get mammograms.

Cappy, my momma, and several of their friends had mastectomies back in the seventies before women had so many options in terms of prostheses. I recall one evening my momma walked in, as the rest of the family was seated at the dining-room table, and asked if we wanted to see her new bosom.

While Daddy turned red, my siblings and I answered enthusiastically, "Yes!" She raised her right arm up over her shoulder and this pointy protrusion, which seconds before had been sitting on the front of her chest, was now resting on her shoulder, pointing straight up at the ceiling.

I thought it'd make great cocktail conversation at the next Cotton Council meeting. My daddy said he wasn't taking my momma to any Cotton Council cocktail party unless she got that bosom under control.

Next she tried one of the silicon pouches, which slips into a pocket in the front of your brassiere. You had to put this silicon bosom thing in a mold at night so it would retain its shape. This worked out pretty well for Momma since it could be confined to a bra and didn't go traveling all over her chest and shoulder.

As a matter of fact it worked so well she began bragging about it to her other one-bosomed friends. The next thing you know, here comes Miss Mary Lee Boatwright, who had a reputation for borrowing clothes for special events rather than buying her own. You got it; Miss Mary Lee appeared for coffee one morning requesting the use of my momma's new bosom. I remember hearing my less-than-generous mother respond, "No, Mary Lee, you get your own bosom." Which she did and happily loaned to everyone who needed it. She was just that kind of sweet person. That bosom rested on the chest of several different Shumard women before it plum wore out. When she finally did retire it, Miss Mary Lee said, "Well, you can only expect so much mileage out of one bosom."

By the time our neighbor, Miss Clareece, had her mastectomy the silicon pouches had become quite common. The only problem with this type of prosthesis was that it would get hot, you know, having that silicon right next to your chest would generate some heat.

One evening Miss Clareece was sitting next to her fireplace reading when her breast/chest grew uncomfortably warm. Just like taking off your shoes and socks will cool you off so will taking off your silicon bosom. So she reached inside her blouse, undid the Velcro pocket, and took the silicon pouch out of the bra. She tossed it in the kindling box and continued reading.

A while later the doorbell rang and she heard her husband, Mr. Jimma, greeting unexpected guests. They soon joined Miss Clareece sitting at the fireplace in the den. She took libation orders and off to the kitchen she went, not giving any thought to the silicon bosom. When she returned with the drinks, she saw, to her horror, that Mr. Jimma was stoking the fire with contents from the kindling box.

"My bosom!" she shrieked as she dropped the tray and dove toward the container. Fortunately, the slick lump of silicon had slid down to the bottom of the pile. The moral of this story is, you better be very careful where you lay your bosom.

Eldon Brice's wife, Miss Anita, wasn't so lucky when her bosom got loose. She was out in the yard picking up sticks when it fell out of her blouse. She liked to wear those kinda low-cut blouses.

Her beagle, Pearl Bailey, came running by and snatched it up in her mouth and took off. A week later when the gardener found Miss Anita's bosom in an iris bed it was punctured and leaking. She put a little duct tape on it and said it was good as new. Miss Anita started wearing turtlenecks after that.

My momma eventually decided she was ready to graduate to an implant. I thought this was quite interesting since she keeps three closets of clothes. One contained size 12, and another size 14, and the third size 16. I wondered what size bosom she was going to have implanted.

When she told my daddy she wanted an implant he

was very supportive and said that would be just fine and he'd be happy to pay for the bosom. She also wanted the bags under her eyes removed. He wasn't really interested in financing that. So she paid for the bags and he paid for the bosom.

With the financial agreement squared away she proceeded with the operation and ever after enjoyed the size 38 breast Dr. Hyde built which sits alongside the God-given size 34 breast. She doesn't seem to mind the imbalance. She says everyone is lopsided, they just won't admit it.

Aunt Cappy seemed to have more trouble with her prosthesis than the other ladies back home. I don't know what Cappy's implant was made of, but it was inflatable and expanded upon a rise in altitude. One time on a plane trip to Denver she thought her left bosom was going to explode as the jet ascended into the clouds.

The man sitting next to her tried to hide behind his *Wall Street Journal* and pretend he didn't notice the missile headed directly toward him. He probably wondered if it did explode would he be injured and if so what kind of insurance would cover such an injury.

Of course, Aunt Cappy noticed him staring and, being the trickster that she is, she leaned in real close. Pressing her missile into his arm, she smiled and whispered, "Lord, this PMS, it can be a killer."

He believed her and leapt from his seat not to return until the flight landed and Aunt Cappy's breast retreated to its assigned seat. As he tried not to look at her now deflating chest she patted his arm, smiled, and shared her philosophy, "That's just like life, now isn't it? You ebb and flow, friends come and go. That's why you should make the most of what God gives you and live your life with great gusto!"